BRIGHT IDEA BOOKS

GARETH
Southgate

Ben Hubbard

raintree

a Capstone company — publishers for children

Raintree is an imprint of Capstone Global Library Limited, a company incorporated in England and Wales having its registered office at 264 Banbury Road, Oxford, OX2 7DY – Registered company number: 6695582

www.raintree.co.uk
myorders@raintree.co.uk

Editor: Helen Cox Cannons
Designer: Justin Hoffmann at Pixelfox
Media researcher: Morgan Walters
Production specialist: Kathy McColley

ISBN 978 1 4747 7712 4 (hardback)
ISBN 978 1 4747 7714 8 (paperback)

British Library Cataloguing in Publication Data
A full catalogue record for this book is available from the British Library.

Acknowledgments
We would like to thank the following for permission to reproduce photographs: Alamy: Allstar Picture Library, 9, 15, PA Images, 7, spread 10-11; Getty Images: Bongarts, 5, Owen Humphreys - PA Images, 13; Newscom: Germany V England/ZUMA Press, 16; Shutterstock: aurielaki, 19, Marco Iacobucci EPP, Cover, 23, 26, Neil Lang, 21, 25, Sergey Nivens, 31.

Every effort has been made to contact copyright holders of material reproduced in this book. Any omissions will be rectified in subsequent printings if notice is given to the publisher.

CONTENTS

CHAPTER 1

FROM FOOTBALLER TO MANAGER

It's 1996. England are playing Germany in the semi-final of the **Euros**. Extra time has ended in a 1–1 draw. A **penalty shootout** will decide the match. Germany scores six penalties and England five.

Now, England defender Gareth Southgate steps forward. He puts the ball on the **spot**. Millions of England fans hold their breath. Gareth shoots. It is saved by the keeper! England are out of the tournament.

Gareth Southgate's saved penalty is every footballer's worst nightmare.

Missing the 1996 penalty haunted Gareth for years afterwards. But, in 2016, he had the chance to make his country proud of him. He was made manager of the England team.

Being England manager comes with a lot of pressure. However, Gareth knew all about footballing pressure. He lived with it for 18 years as a player.

BAD MEMORIES

"It will never be off my back, sadly. That's something that will live with me forever."
Gareth Southgate, on the 1996 penalty

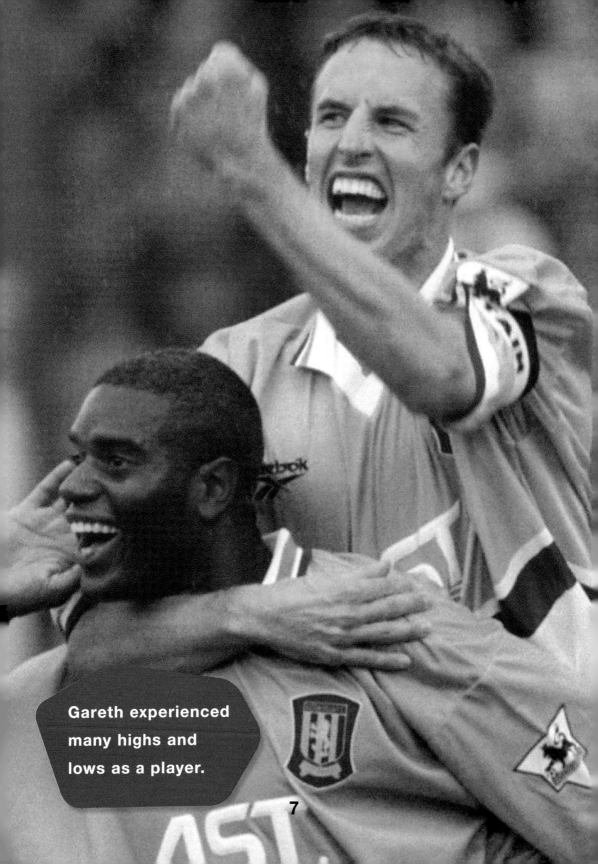

Gareth experienced
many highs and
lows as a player.

7

CHAPTER 2

GARETH'S PLAYING CAREER

Gareth Southgate was born in 1970. He joined Crystal Palace as a player in 1988. He was polite and eager to learn. He was also a natural leader. He was always made team captain. Soon other clubs wanted to sign Gareth. He joined Aston Villa in 1995 and Middlesbrough in 2001.

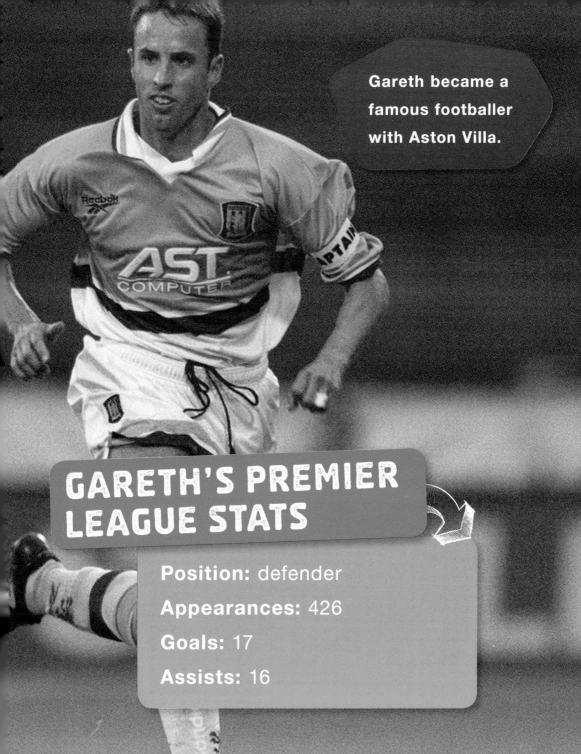

Gareth became a famous footballer with Aston Villa.

GARETH'S PREMIER LEAGUE STATS

Position: defender

Appearances: 426

Goals: 17

Assists: 16

In 1995, Gareth got an exciting phone call. He had been chosen for the England team. Over time, Gareth became a key England player.

Gareth and David Beckham played for England together.

As a player, Gareth played 57 times for England. He played at the Euros in 1996 and 2000. He also played at the 1998 and 2002 World Cups.

CHAPTER 3

GARETH'S COACHING CAREER

In 2006 Gareth got ready to retire from football. Footballers usually stop playing in their thirties. Gareth wondered what he would do next. Then, an opportunity came up.

The Middlesbrough manager, Steve McClaren, had left to manage the England team. Now Middlesbrough needed a new manager. Gareth was offered the job. Some said Gareth wouldn't be any good. He wasn't even a qualified coach. But Gareth wanted to try.

Gareth kicked his last ball as a player in 2006.

Gareth was **determined** to be a good manager at Middlesbrough. His first season in charge was a success. Middlesbrough finished in 12th place in the Premier League table. There are 20 places in total. In one match, Middlesbrough even beat Manchester City 8–1.

Gareth was Middlesbrough manager for three seasons.

Things went downhill for Gareth after that. In 2009, Middlesbrough were **relegated** from the Premier League. This meant they would play in a lower league the next season. That October, Gareth was sacked.

Gareth agreed to manage the England team for four matches.

After Middlesbrough, Gareth worked as a football **pundit**. Pundits are paid to discuss football matches on television. Then, in 2013, there was good news for Gareth. He was asked to manage the England Under-21 team.

In 2016 there was a big **scandal**. The manager of the England team suddenly resigned. Gareth was asked if he would take over as a **caretaker manager**. He jumped at the chance.

CHAPTER 4

ENGLAND MANAGER

Some people thought Gareth would make a bad caretaker manager. They said his Middlesbrough team had been relegated. Others remembered Gareth's missed penalty in 1996. Gareth wanted to prove them all wrong. But he only had four matches to do it. Also, these matches were World Cup **qualifiers**. England could not afford to lose. Soon, the results were in.

WORLD CUP QUALIFIER RESULTS

England 2–0 **Malta**

England 0–0 **Slovenia**

England 3–0 **Scotland**

England 2–2 **Spain**

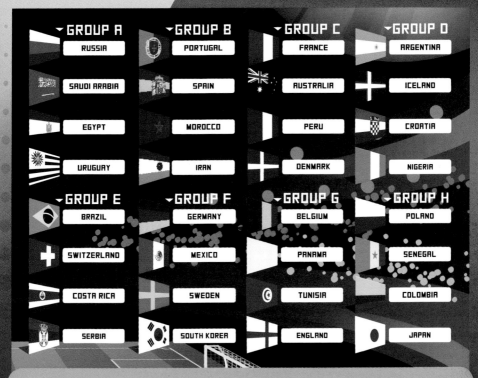

▼GROUP A	▼GROUP B	▼GROUP C	▼GROUP D
RUSSIA	PORTUGAL	FRANCE	ARGENTINA
SAUDI ARABIA	SPAIN	AUSTRALIA	ICELAND
EGYPT	MOROCCO	PERU	CROATIA
URUGUAY	IRAN	DENMARK	NIGERIA

▼GROUP E	▼GROUP F	▼GROUP G	▼GROUP H
BRAZIL	GERMANY	BELGIUM	POLAND
SWITZERLAND	MEXICO	PANAMA	SENEGAL
COSTA RICA	SWEDEN	TUNISIA	COLOMBIA
SERBIA	SOUTH KOREA	ENGLAND	JAPAN

This chart shows the countries that played in the World Cup and their groups. England were in Group G.

Gareth's skill as England manager surprised everyone. His matches as caretaker manager had been a big success. England had qualified for the 2018 World Cup in Russia. Bigger news followed. Gareth was made the permanent England manager.

People suddenly became interested in Gareth. He was well-spoken and loved wearing waistcoats. But England had not won the World Cup since 1966. They had not even reached the semi-finals since 1990. Few fans expected much from Gareth and his team.

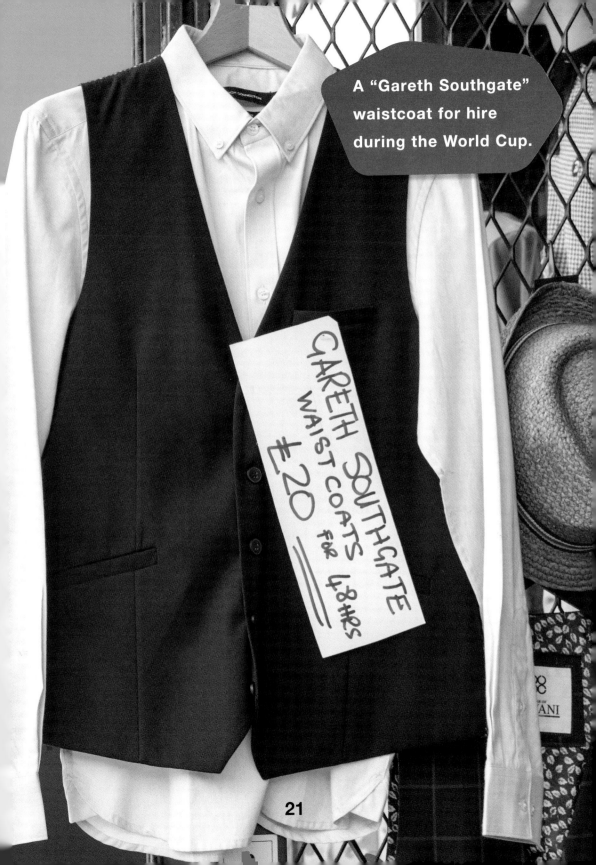

A "Gareth Southgate" waistcoat for hire during the World Cup.

21

CHAPTER 5

THE 2018 WORLD CUP

England made a good start at the World Cup. They beat Tunisia and Panama. Now they faced Colombia in the knock-out stage. To reach the quarter-final, England had to win. But after 120 minutes the score was 1–1. The match would be decided by a penalty shootout.

Penalties brought back bad memories for Gareth. England had lost many tournaments this way. But not on this day. England won the shootout 4–3!

England captain Harry Kane scored with his penalty.

England did not stop with their win over Colombia. The team then beat Sweden in the quarter-finals. England had reached its first semi-final in 28 years! The team only needed two more victories to win the World Cup.

England fans caught World Cup fever. People supported Gareth by wearing waistcoats. Waistcoat sales shot up in England. Children even wore them to school. People couldn't wait for the semi-final against Croatia.

London's Southgate tube station was temporarily renamed "Gareth Southgate" station.

Over 26 million people in Britain watched the World Cup semi-final on television. It was a tough match. After 90 minutes, the score was 1–1. Croatia then scored in **extra time**. England was out of the World Cup!

England fans were devastated. But they said Gareth had made them proud of their footballers. Gareth was given a new contract until 2022. Today, he has won the respect of fans and critics alike.

"I'm remarkably proud of the group of players."
Gareth Southgate

GLOSSARY

assist
move which leads to another player scoring a goal

caretaker manager
manager that takes over a team for a temporary period

determine
making a firm decision about something and sticking to it

Euros
UEFA (Union of European Football Associations) European Championship, which is held every four years

extra time
an additional 30 minutes of play added to a cup match that ends in a draw

penalty shootout
deciding a match through penalties when there is no winning team after normal play

pundit
someone who gives their professional opinion about football matches on television

qualifier
match a team has to win to be allowed to join a tournament

relegate
when a team is moved to a lower league after losing too many matches

scandal
event involving wrongdoing that causes great outrage

spot
mark, 11 metres (12 yards) from the goal, that a penalty kick is taken from

TIMELINE

1970: Gareth Southgate is born in Watford, England.

1988–1995: Gareth plays for Crystal Palace.

1995–2001: Gareth plays for Aston Villa.

1995–2004: Gareth plays for the England Team.

2001–2006: Gareth plays for Middlesbrough Football Club after signing for a £6 million fee.

2006: Gareth becomes manager of Middlesbrough.

2013–2016: Gareth manages the England Under-21 team.

2016: Gareth is named caretaker England manager and then permanent England manager.

2018: England reach the World Cup semi-finals. Gareth is given a new contract until 2022.

ACTIVITY

WOULD YOU LIKE TO WORK AS A FOOTBALL COMMENTATOR?

Commentators are the people who describe what is happening during a match on television. Why not try being a commentator during a match? You can do this by turning down the sound on a television or laptop and giving your own commentary. You can discuss certain players as well as describing the action.

Most matches have two commentators. You could ask a friend to join you. When you get good you could commentate on a match for your friends or family.

FIND OUT MORE

Love reading about football? Learn more here:

Books

Football (Fantastic Sport Facts), Michael Hurley (Raintree, 2013)

Football: Rules, Equipment and Key Playing Tips (First Facts: First Sports Facts), Danielle S. Hammelef (Raintree, 2017)

Spotlight on the World Cup (Young Explorer), Chris Oxlade (Raintree 2017)

Websites

On the English Football Association website you can find out about footballers in the England team:
www.thefa.com

The English Premier League website provides information about games and players:
www.premierleague.com

INDEX